ALPHABET SCRAMBLE

By Jeeline L. Hilaire

Illustrations by Derrick J. Thomas

BK

ROYSTON
Publishing

BK Royston Publishing LLC
P. O. Box 4321
Jeffersonville, IN 47131
http://www.bkroystonpublishing.com
bkroystonpublishing@gmail.com

Cover Design: Derrick Thomas
Illustrations: Derrick Thomas

ISBN-13: 978-1-946111-41-8

Printed in the USA

DEDICATION

For my lovely niece Adrielle, my handsome nephew Jathan, my future children and YOU.

ACKNOWLEDGEMENT

I would like to give my Lord, Jesus Christ all the glory and honor for instilling in me the idea and making this dream become a reality. To my parents Marie and Ernest Hilaire, thank you for your support. Marcda, my "sissy pooh", I love you so much. Last but not least, my circle of influence, you all are amazing, thank you. Thanks to everyone (too many too name, you know who you are) who supported me in every way to make this become a reality. I love all of you and may God bless you!

Dear Parents, Grandparents, Siblings, Guardians and Educators:

I know many of you are wondering why this book is called "Alphabet Scramble" and why the letters aren't in order. Well, in my experience in the Early Childhood field, it became apparent early on that learning the alphabet song is quite simple for most children. The problem is when it comes to recognizing each letter separately, not every child is able to name the letters while they are out of order. Because of that, I chose to adapt a new method to not teach the alphabet in order because I wanted my students to know and recognize the letters not just know the ABC song. That is why this book is titled "Alphabet Scramble." It has worked even with my two year old niece who is able to recognize the letters. My niece is one of the featured characters, the other is my nephew. As you read this book to your loved ones, I ask that you're patient and understand that each child learns at his or her own pace. Please send me your success stories, I would love to hear from you. Enjoy teaching the alphabet in a fun new way!

Sincerely, Jeeline L. Hilaire

I is for "Ice Cream"

2

E is for "Elephant"

U is for "Umbrella"

4

A is for "Aunt"

Q is for "Quilt"

M is for "Mangos"

N is for "Nest"

B is for "Butterflies"

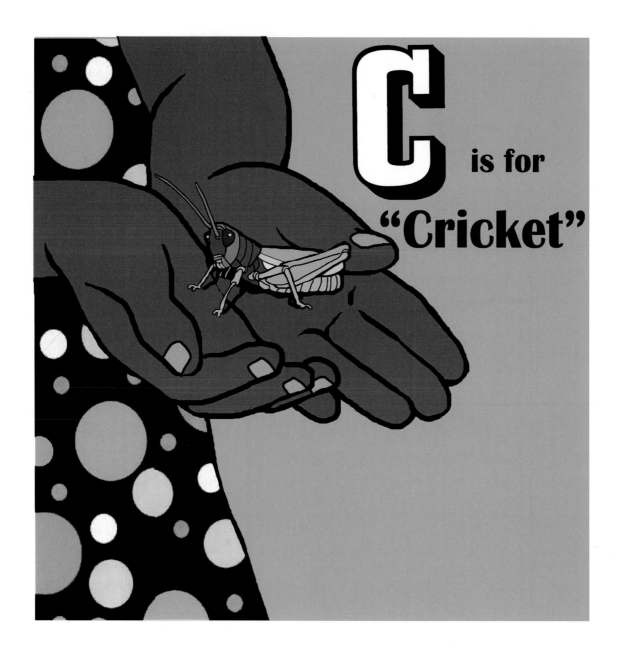

C is for "Cricket"

L is for "Love"

H is for "Helicopter"

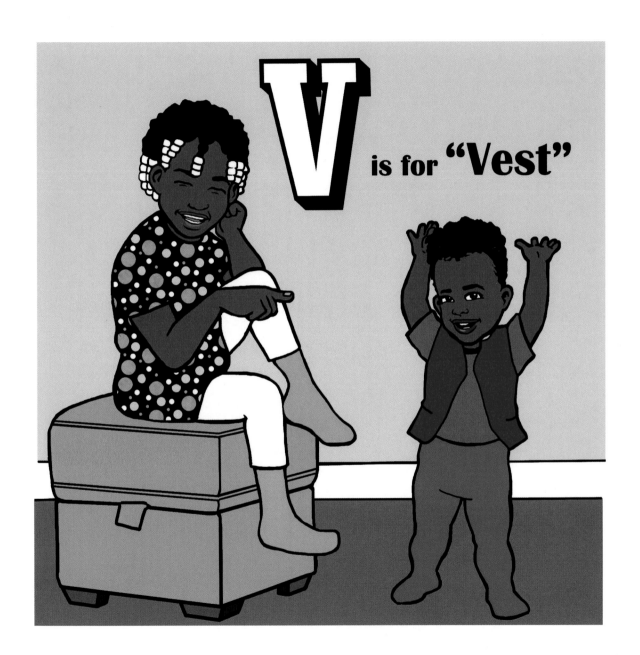

V is for "Vest"

19

G is for "GrandMother"

W is for "Wagon"

About the Author

Affectionately known as Ms. Jee, Jeeline was born in La Gonave, Haiti to Ernest and Marie on December 26, 1989. She was raised in West Palm Beach, Florida. She attended West-ward Elementary School, Roosevelt Middle School (class of 2004), Inlet Grove Community High School (class of 2008) and Palm Beach State College where she received her Early Childhood Degree and other certifications. Jeeline always had a passion for children, but she was scared to follow her heart because growing up a nurse is what everyone thought she would be.

In 2012, her older sister Marcda, asked her "Jee why do you want to be a nurse?" She was silenced and Marcda said, "If it's because you like kids, you're in the wrong field." At that very moment, tears ran down her cheeks. She knew she was in the wrong field because nursing isn't fun and games with children (neither is early childhood, but fun is part of teaching). That semester she changed her major. Immediately, her heart found its home as she started learning on how to become a better educator. Jeeline has worked in private and public preschools and soon she will have her own childcare. She also has staff credentials and director's credentials. At her church, Philadelphia Church of the Newborns she serves as director of the Children/Youth Sunday School Director and Program Coordinator on the Executive Board of Girl's Talk Ministry. Jeeline, still resides in West Palm Beach, Florida where she continues pursuing her passion for teaching as she changes lives step by according to God's purpose and will. She hopes to have a family of her own one day to enjoy "Alphabet Scramble" and all other ventures.

Ms. Jeeline and her niece Adrielle "Emmy Bear" at Build A Bear.

Ms. Jeeline and her nephew Jathan (her superman) striking a pose for their daily picture.

"Smiles and Silly Faces are Priceless Jewels Worth Sharing." JLH